Non-Fiction Titles by Janvier T. Chando
ICONS AND VILLAINS: Recent Political Assassinations…
FALLEN HEROES: African Leaders Whose Assassinations…
UKRAINE: The Tug-of-War Between Russia and the West
Cameroon: France's Dysfunctional Puppet System in Africa
Cameroon: The Haunted Heart of Africa

Fiction Titles by Janvier Chando
The Usurper: and Other Stories
Triple Agent, Double Cross
Disciples of Fortune
The Union Moujik
Flash of the Sun
Fortune Calls
Fortune's Master
The Girl on the Trail
Fortune's Children
The Norilsk Bears
Me Before Them
The Grandmothers and Perfect Love
The Fire and Ice Legend
The Sweetest Madness
The Hunger Fire
The Shades of Fire
Father and Sons
Fateful Ties
The Verdict of Hades
His Majesty's Trial
Ngoko's Folly
The Usurper
The Dowry
I am Hated
The Oaf

Upcoming Titles by Janvier Chando
The Home Drifters
The Mortal Friends
The White Hawk
The Norilsk Bears

THE DEATH THAT STRANGLED THE HEART OF AFRICA:

The Dehumanizing Assassination of Patrice Lumumba of Congo and the Derailment of the former Belgian Colony

Janvier T. Chando

TISI BOOKS

NEW YORK, RALEIGH, LONDON, AMSTERDAM

THE DEATH THAT STRANGLED THE HEART OF AFRICA: The Dehumanizing Assassination of Patrice Lumumba of Congo and the Derailment of the former Belgian Colony

ISBN-13: 978-1-9735-1463-3
ISBN-10: 1-9735-1463-X

PUBLISHED BY TISI BOOKS
www.tisibooks.com

NEW YORK, RALEIGH, LONDON, AMSTERDAM

Printed in The United States of America

Acknowledgement

Special words of appreciation to Aunty Anna Mapajane Chitja for introducing me to the Lumumba legacy.

Dedication

The book is dedicated to all iconic and legendary leaders whose purposes were to serve humanity and advance the wellbeing of mankind, especially those who were cut short in their historic missions by the evil forces of this world.

THE DEATH THAT STRANGLED THE HEART OF AFRICA:

The Dehumanizing Assassination of Patrice Lumumba of Congo and the Derailment of the former Belgian Colony

Patrice Lumumba Quotes

"The colonialists care nothing for Africa for her own sake. They are attracted by African riches and their actions are guided by the desire to preserve their interests in Africa against the wishes of the African people. For the colonialists all means are good if they help them to possess these riches."

"The day will come when history will speak. But it will not be the history which will be taught in Brussels, Paris, Washington or the United Nations…Africa will write its own history and in both north and south, it will be a history of glory and dignity."

"Political independence has no meaning if it is not accompanied by rapid economic and social development."

"Without dignity there is no liberty, without justice there is no dignity, and without independence there are no free men."

"A minimum of comfort is necessary for the practice of virtue."

"The only thing which we wanted for our country is the right to a worthy life, to dignity without pretense, to independence without restrictions. This was never the desire of the Belgian colonialists and their Western allies…"

"These divisions, which the colonial powers have always exploited the better to dominate us, have played an important role — and are still playing that role — in the suicide of Africa."

We know that Africa is neither French, nor British, nor American, nor Russian, that it is African. We know the objects of the West. Yesterday they divided us on the level of a tribe, clan and village…They want to create antagonistic blocs, satellites…"

"No one is perfect in this imperfect world."

"African unity and solidarity are no longer dreams. They must be expressed in decisions."

Contents

Acknowledgement 7

Dedication 9

Patrice Lumumba Quotes 13

MAPS 19

INTRODUCTION 23

Chapter One 25

Chapter Two... 29

Chapter Three... 34

Chapter Four 38

Contents

Acknowledgement 7

Dedication 9

Patrice Lumumba Quotes.. 13

MAPS... 19

INTRODUCTION 23

Chapter One 25

Chapter Two... 29

Chapter Three.. 34

Chapter Four 38

MAPS

Congo on a Map of the World

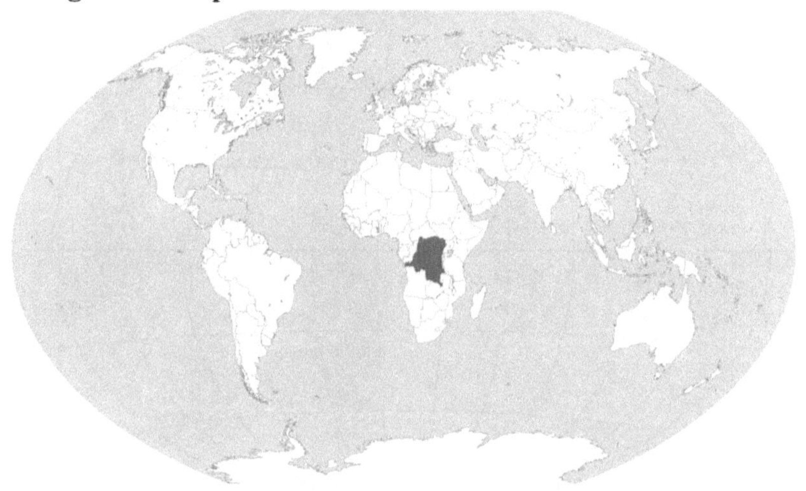

Administrative Map of the Democratic Republic of Congo, 1960

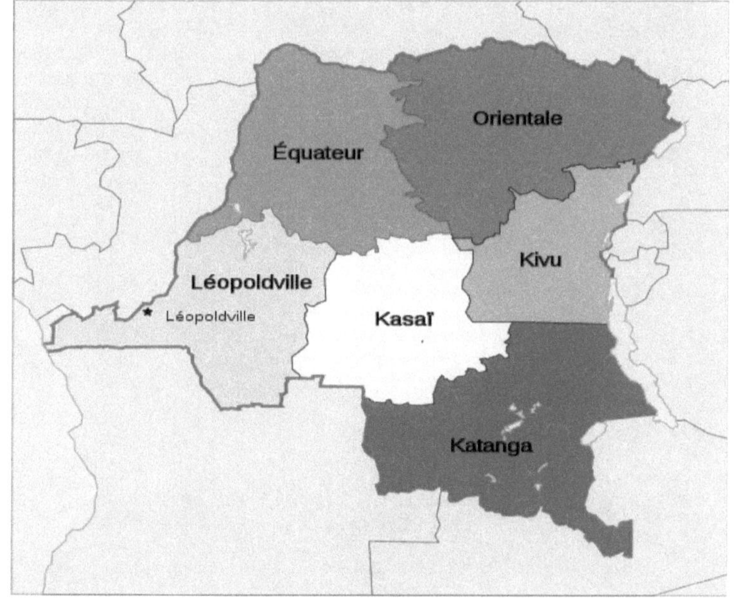

Administrative Map of the Democratic Republic of Congo, 2019

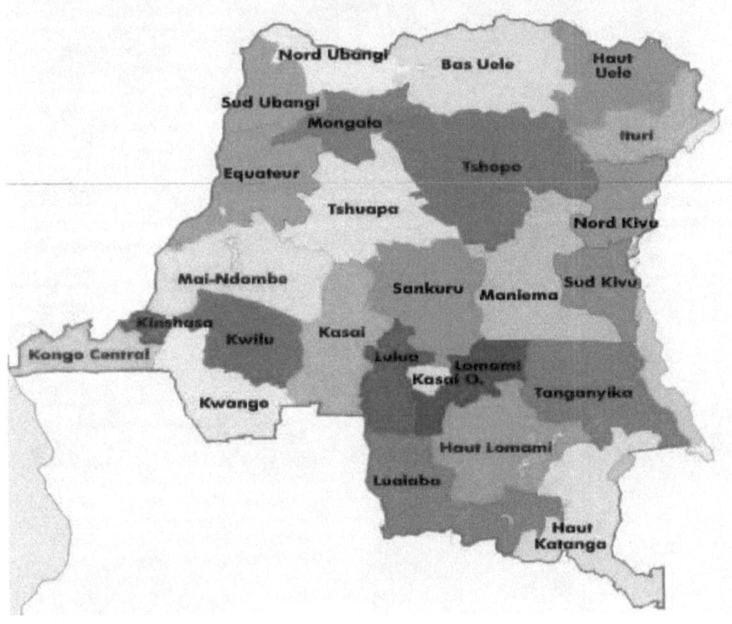

Democracy in Africa

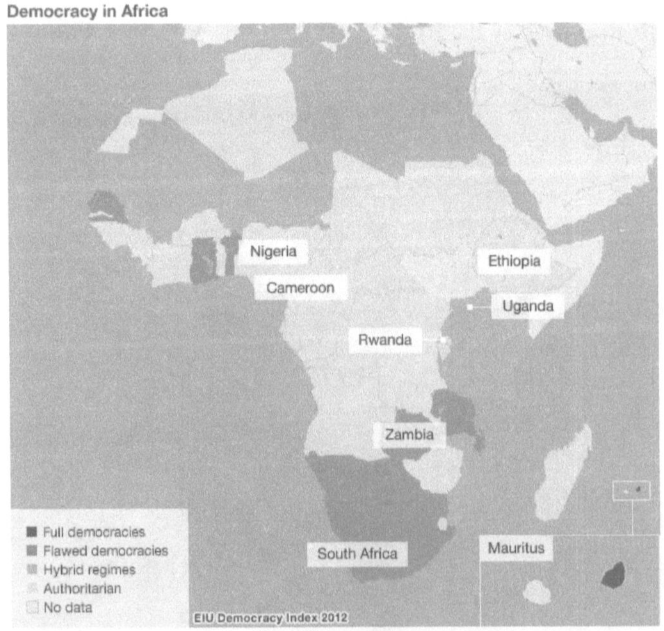

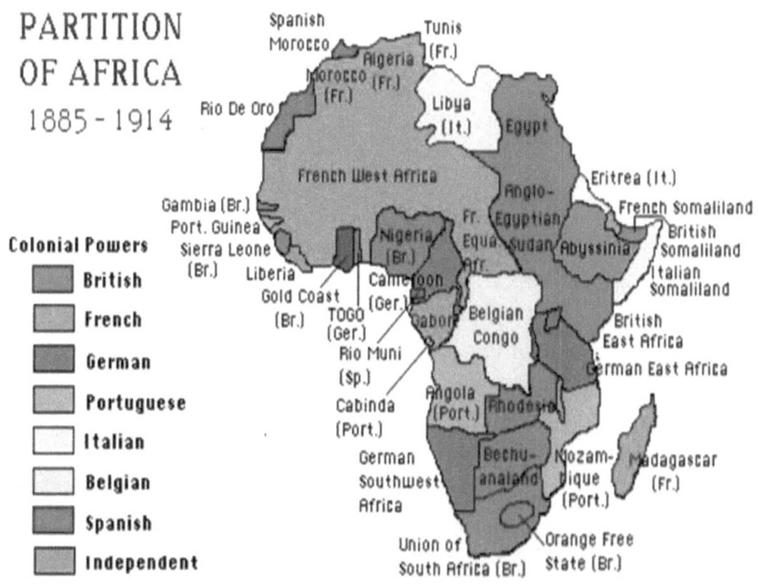

PARTITION
OF AFRICA
1885 - 1914

Colonial Powers
British
French
German
Portuguese
Italian
Belgian
Spanish
Independent

Spanish Morocco
Tunis (Fr.)
Algeria (Fr.)
Morocco (Fr.)
Libya (It.)
Rio De Oro
Egypt
French West Africa
Eritrea (It.)
Gambia (Br.)
Anglo-Egyptian
French Somaliland
Port. Guinea
Fr. Equa. Afr.
Egyptian Sudan
British Somaliland
Sierra Leone (Br.)
Nigeria (Br.)
Abyssinia
Italian Somaliland
Liberia
Cameroon (Ger.)
Gold Coast (Br.)
TOGO (Ger.)
Gabon
Belgian Congo
British East Africa
Rio Muni (Sp.)
German East Africa
Cabinda (Port.)
Angola (Port.)
Rhodesia
German Southwest Africa
Bechuanaland
Mozambique (Port.)
Madagascar (Fr.)
Union of South Africa (Br.)
Orange Free State (Br.)

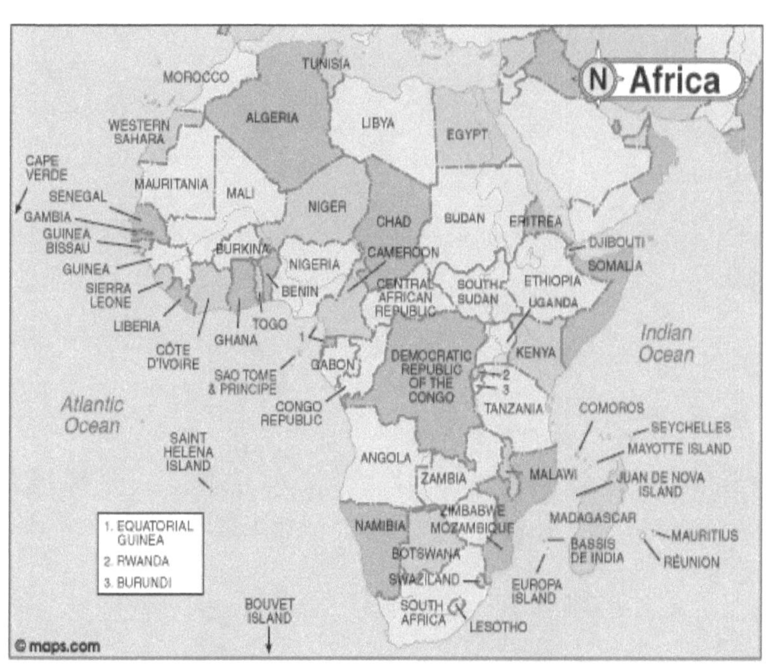

N Africa
MOROCCO
TUNISIA
ALGERIA
LIBYA
EGYPT
WESTERN SAHARA
CAPE VERDE
MAURITANIA
MALI
NIGER
CHAD
SUDAN
ERITREA
SENEGAL
GAMBIA
GUINEA BISSAU
BURKINA
DJIBOUTI
GUINEA
NIGERIA
CAMEROON
SOMALIA
SIERRA LEONE
BENIN
CENTRAL AFRICAN REPUBLIC
SOUTH SUDAN
ETHIOPIA
LIBERIA
TOGO
UGANDA
GHANA
CÔTE D'IVOIRE
GABON
DEMOCRATIC REPUBLIC OF THE CONGO
KENYA
SAO TOME & PRINCIPE
Indian Ocean
CONGO REPUBLIC
TANZANIA
COMOROS
Atlantic Ocean
SAINT HELENA ISLAND
SEYCHELLES
MAYOTTE ISLAND
ANGOLA
JUAN DE NOVA ISLAND
ZAMBIA
MALAWI
MADAGASCAR
ZIMBABWE
MAURITIUS
NAMIBIA
MOZAMBIQUE
BASSIS DE INDIA
RÉUNION
BOTSWANA
SWAZILAND
EUROPA ISLAND
BOUVET ISLAND
SOUTH AFRICA
LESOTHO
1. EQUATORIAL GUINEA
2. RWANDA
3. BURUNDI
© maps.com

INTRODUCTION

In my search for the answer to why certain geopolitical flashpoints exist in the world, in my pry to know the reason(s) why some countries and the world in general experienced sudden and dramatic changes that led to war, instability or a reorientation of their domestic and foreign policies that not only affected these countries but also influence certain regions or the whole world, I explored political assassinations over the past dozens of decades that changed our world. By our world, I mean our communities, countries, regions and humanity as a whole.

In treating the different assassinations that took place over the years, I used an approach characterized by political sociology, where I succinctly analyzed the historical and social factors that not only led to the assassinations, but that also arose from the killing of these historical figures. And from these factors, we are presented with an idea or pictures of how the society affected has evolved since the traumatic event(s).

From the backlashes that followed the assassination of historic, legendary or iconic figures, we can learn something useful and come up with scenarios or what to expect as calamities if particular leaders are assassinated, and so act accordingly in preventing their assassinations.

Chapter One

Syria is bad enough, it's a pretty terrible atrocity. But there are much worse ones in the world. So, for example, the worst atrocities in the past decade have been in the Congo, the Eastern Congo, where maybe 5 million people have been killed.

Noam Chomsky — October 8, 2013

Patrice Lumumba

Patrice Lumumba shortly before his death

The January 17, 1961 assassination of Patrice Lumumba, the first democratically elected prime minister of what is today the Democratic Republic of the Congo (DRC), is considered by many Africans as "the most important assassination of the 20th century" because it not only wrecked the country, but it also polarized and paralyzed Africa, resulting in a disunity that the continent has yet to recover from. This heinous crime was a culmination of two inter-related assassination plots by elements within the American and Belgian governments that made use of Congolese accomplices and a Belgian execution squad to carry out the slaying of the leader of this infant nation in the heart of Africa that just got its independence from Belgium on 30 June 1960.

Historians, sociologists, and geopolitical pundits all agree that Congo is the most traumatized country in Africa and the world, and that of all the atrocities that Congo experienced in its abused history, Patrice Lumumba's assassination was the single cruelest act. In fact, it is rightly viewed as the country's original sin.

The assassination took place less than seven months after the independence of this territory occupying 7.7% of the landmass of Africa. The act transformed into a stumbling block to the hopes of implementing the lofty ideals of Congolese national unity, material prosperity, democracy, economic independence, liberty, and pan-African solidarity that Lumumba had been championing. What cannot be overlooked in particular is the fact that his assassination served as a shattering blow to the hopes, dreams, and aspirations of millions of Congolese, and it disillusioned an even greater number of Africans across the continent.

The fact that one of the Soviet Union's largest universities — The Peoples' Friendship University of Russia — that was founded on February 05, 1960, got renamed "The Patrice Lumumba University" on February 22, 1961, and the fact that this institution of higher learning went on to educate close to a hundred thousand foreigners, most of them Africans, highlights the historical significance of the young African's death to Africa and the rest of the world during the Cold War.

As it turns out, the assassination's historical importance

lies in a multitude of factors, of which the most relevant at the time were based on:

- the global context in which it took place (President Eisenhower authorized the assassination and the CIA carried out his abduction and transfer; the United Nations, its Secretary-General Dag Hammarskjöld, the Soviet Union and the British M16 were involved in the tragedy; and the Belgians directed his murder and those of his two associates (allies Maurice Mpolo and Joseph Okito) before later getting rid of the bodies by digging them up and dissolving them in sulfuric acid, and then grinding and scattering the bones)

- its impact on Congolese politics since then,

- and Lumumba's overall legacy as a civic-nationalist leader and pan-Africanist icon. After all, he was working with Félix Moumié, the Cameroonian liberation movement leader that the French Secret Service (SDECE) poisoned in Geneva, Switzerland on 3 November 3, 1960.

Chapter Two

One question that has been prevalent in the geopolitical sphere is this:

Why did the USA, Britain, France, and Belgium get involved in the assassination of Congo's first democratically elected leader?

It all began in April 1884, seven months before the Berlin Congress, when the United States of America became the first country in the world to recognize the claims of the Belgian King Leopold II to the territories of the Congo Basin. These territories became known as the Congo Free State. King Leopold II ruled it as his private property, making use of a small cadre of white administrators that were drawn from across Europe.

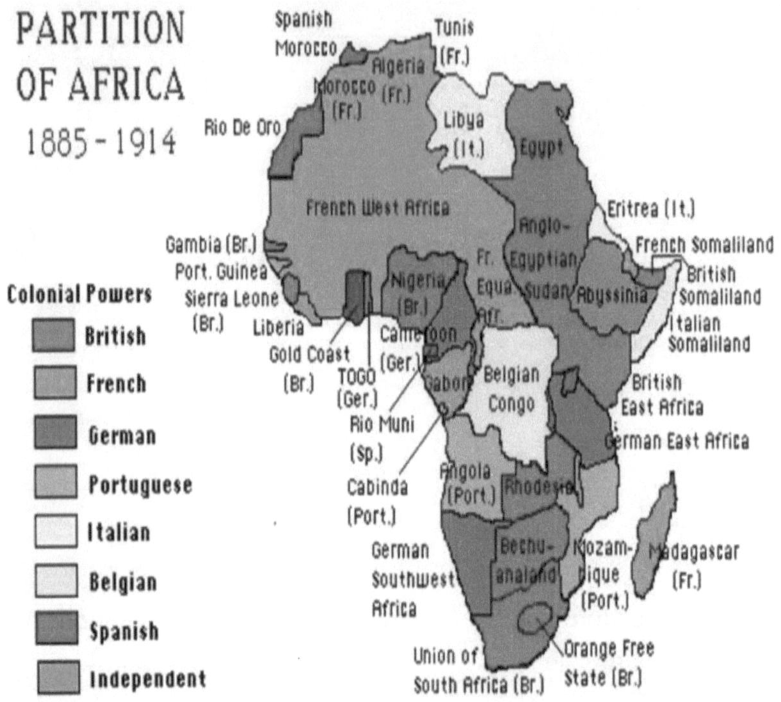

The Congo Free State made King Leopold II one of the wealthiest monarchs in the world, an outsized accomplishment, given the fact that he was the king of Belgium, which was such a small country in the neighborhood of mighty geopolitical entities like the British, German, Russian and Austro-Hungarian Empires. But the Belgian king's wealth was accumulated at an enormous cost to the native African population as the people were forced to provide unpaid labor that was not different from slavery, in the exploitation of the land's mineral, forest and agricultural resources for the Belgian monarch. However, when the atrocities related to the brutal economic exploitation in King Leopold's Congo Free State resulted in millions of fatalities, the United States of America joined other world powers and forced the Belgian state to take over the Congo Free State as a regular colony and stop the killings and maiming of the native Congolese population — a genocide per se.

It was only after Congo got transformed into a regular colony that the United States of America acquired a strategic stake in the enormous natural wealth of the territory. In fact, the USA used the uranium from Congolese mines to manufacture the first atomic weapons that were used on the Japanese cities of Hiroshima and Nagasaki, leading to an abrupt end of the Second World War in the Pacific.

The strategic importance of resources-rich Congo in particular, and resource-rich Africa in general, especially in helping the Allies win the Second World War, became a curse afterward when the continent sought independence from its colonial masters. This was at a time that the Cold War was dominating geopolitics. America and its Western allies resolved to give the colonies independence all right, but not the type of independence the rest of the world knew about. The Western powers were not prepared to let the people of the African colonies have effective control over the strategic raw materials in their territories, for fear that these assets could fall into the hands of the countries of the Soviet or communist camp. That was why western interests perceived a threat in Patrice Lumumba's resolve to achieve genuine independence for Congo and to gain full control over the country's resources for use in developing the infant nation and in improving the living conditions of the

Congolese people.

The Natural Resources of the Central African Region

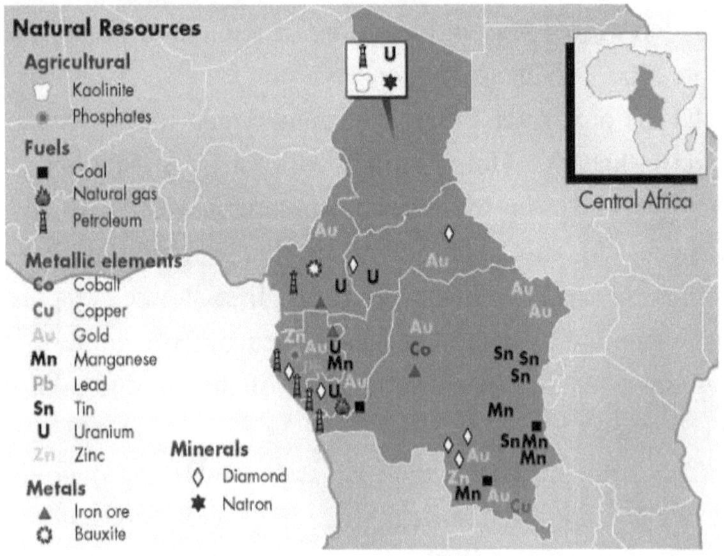

To stop Patrice Lumumba, the United States of America and Belgium left no stone unturned, including the use of the United Nations Secretariat under Dag Hammarskjöld and Ralph Bunche, the buying of the support of Lumumba's Congolese rivals, the silencing of some African leaders who had been supportive of Lumumba and the pan-Africanist goal he shared, and the buying of the services of killers for hire (mercenaries) to eliminate the obstacle to their smooth control of Congo, a country that they intended to be nothing but a quasi-independent state that is subservient to western leaders, the Western countries and western interests.

Colonization of Africa and Dates of Independence

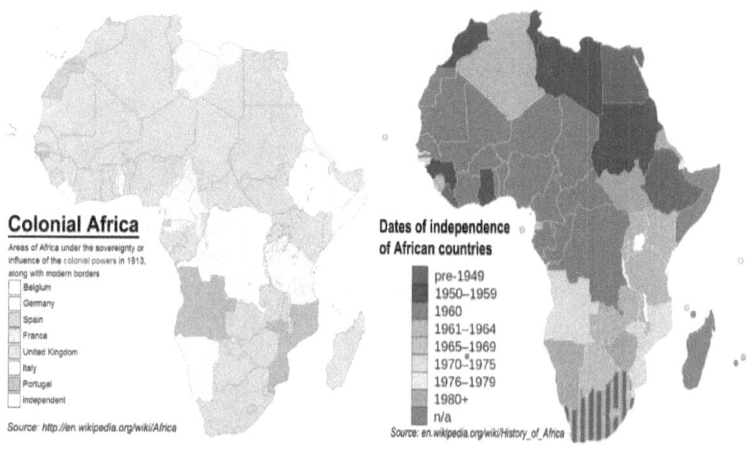

Chapter Three

Right after granting independence to Congo on June 30, 1960, Belgium and its western allies went about undermining the infant nation's stability by encouraging a virulent opposition to Lumumba's government, using western-backed Congolese politicians. In fact, by December 1960, Congo was effectively under four separate governments, three of which were under the thumbs of the anti-Lumumba factions backed by Western Powers. These were:

- the central government in the Congolese capital of Léopoldville (Kinshasa)
- a rival central government established by Lumumba's followers in Stanleyville (Kisangani)
- a secessionist regime in the mineral-rich province of Katanga under the leadership of Moise Tshombe
- and another secessionist administration in the South Kasai province under the leadership of Albert Kalonji.

With Lumumba liquidated half a year after the granting of independence to Congo, with the removal of what the

Western geopolitical players perceived as the major threat to their interests in the new country, Belgium, Britain, France, and the United States of America led international efforts to spread the authority of the moderate and pro-western regime in Kinshasa over the entire Congo. It was a two-pronged strategy involving the use of the new Western-created Congolese army under the command of the Western-backed regime of Mobutu Sese Seko and the use of United Nations peacekeepers. The strategy was so effective that the Lumumbist stronghold in the East of the country centered around Kisangani, fell in August 1961. South Kasai region capitulated in September 1962, and the secession of the Katanga region was reversed in January 1963.

The 1960-1961 Congo Crisis

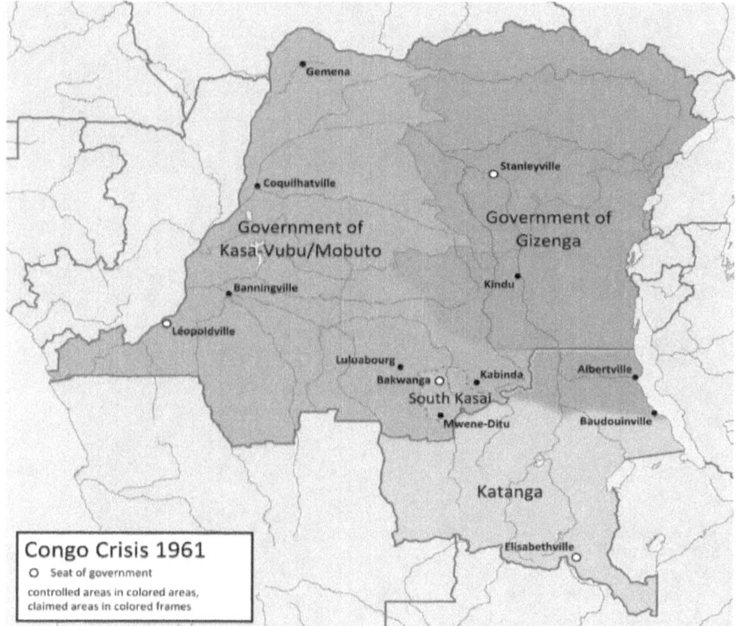

After wrecking the newly independent Congo in order to undermine Lumumba, after assassinating Lumumba and installing a puppet government, and then directing it in uniting and stabilizing the country again, the Western powers were surprised when a radical social movement for a "second independence" arose, challenging the neocolonial state and its pro-western leadership. It was a mass movement of workers, lower civil servants, the urban unemployed, peasants, and students. They were provided leadership by Lumumba's lieutenants, most of whom had regrouped in the former French Congolese capital of Brazzaville, across the Congo River from the former Belgian Congolese capital city of Kinshasa.

The 1964 Simba Rebellion

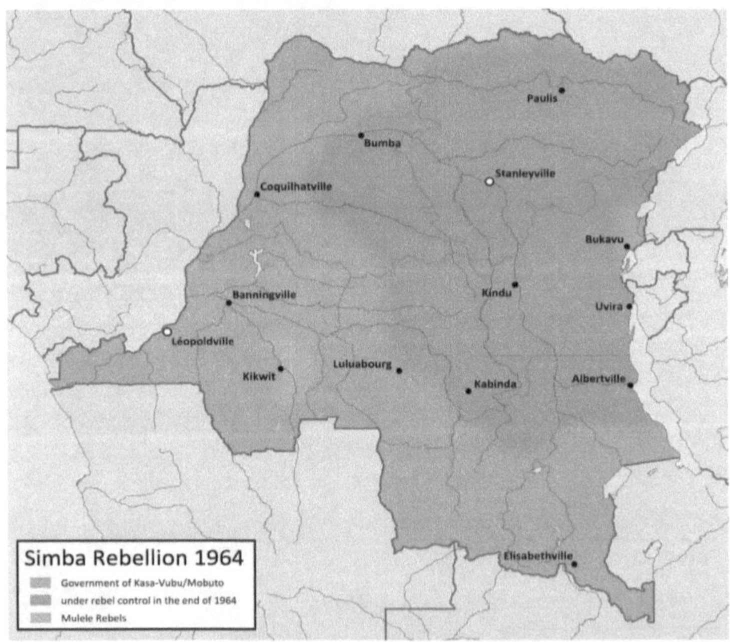

In October 1963, these Lumumbists established a National Liberation Council (CNL) with a mission to oust the Mobutu regime and create a New Congo. They were taken seriously to the point where the Soviet Union gave them military assistance. Some of the few surviving pan-Africanist governments in the continent provided support as well. Even Ernesto Che Guevara, the Argentine revolutionary icon and second in command of Fidel Castro of Cuba, set up a base in the Congo to help these Lumumbists and anti-neocolonialists. In fact, when Che Guevara wrote in 1964 that:

> *"We must move forward, striking out tirelessly against imperialism. From all over the world, we have to learn lessons which events afford. Lumumba's murder should be a lesson for all of us…",*

he began the immortalization of Patrice Lumumba after failing in his Congo expedition to galvanize the Lumumbists against the Western puppet regime of Mobutu Sese Seko who not only impoverished Congo during his three-and-a-half-decade rule, but who also became richer than the country he misruled.

Chapter Four

In all the continents of the world today, streets, parks, squares, airports, statues and other infrastructures abound that bear the name Lumumba in honor of an altruist, a man who embraced a more advanced form of civic-nationalism called union-nationalism, who opposed the division of his country along ethnic or regional lines, and who supported pan-Africanism and the liberation of all the colonial territories not only in Africa, but also in the rest of the world.

Patrice Lumumba's legacy continues to serve as an inspiration in Congolese politics today, as dozens of political parties proclaim their belief in his ideas of "Positive Neutralism," which advocates a return to African values and which rejects any imported ideology, including the ideology of the Soviet Union:

"We are not Communists or Catholics. We are African nationalists," Patrice Lumumba once said.

Pan-Africanists (those who dream of a future African Economic Union with an integrated political system and military structure) cherish the Lumumba legacy and place him alongside Kwame Nkrumah of Ghana, Sekou Touré of Guinea, Julius Nyerere of Tanzania and the leaders of the historic UPC party of Cameroon — who got liquidated during their fight against French colonialism and neocolonialism that led to the country's unification and independence — as the icons of Africa's independence-struggle era that sowed the seeds for the African Union, which is yet to be realized.

On May 31, 1997, a Lumumbist made it to power after leading a full-scale rebellion against the rule of the ailing Mobutu under the banner of the Alliance of Democratic Forces for the Liberation of Congo-Zaire (ADFL), and with support from Rwanda, Uganda and Burundi, thereby marking the end of the First Congo War in a feat that took the ADFL just half a year to sweep across the country, a territory that is slightly more than half the size of the European Union. Laurent-Désiré Kabila, as Mobuto's nemesis or new president was called, made a powerful statement when he changed the name of the country from Zaire to the Democratic Republic of the Congo, which is how the central African nation was known from 1964-1971.

Laurent-Désiré Kabila did not come from nowhere. As a matter of fact, by 1965, he had emerged as the most distinguished of the late Patrice Lumumba's lieutenants following the early 1960s Congo Crisis and the rebellion against Mobutu Sese Sekou that followed it. He was even acknowledged by Che Guevara during his Congo expedition, even though the Argentine revolutionary thought his Congolese counterpart was too distracted at the time, concluding that he was "not the man of the hour".

Even though Laurent Kabila's former allies (Rwanda, Uganda, and Burundi) would turn against him a year later, and back a new rebellion against his rule under the banner of the Rally for Congolese Democracy (RCD), thereby sparking off the Second Congo War that saw him lose control of Eastern Congo, the Lumumba legacy prevailed as he held onto the south and west of the country with assistance from Angola, Namibia, and Zimbabwe. Laurent Kabila would be shot and killed by his guard on January 01, 2001, a year and a half after the withdrawal of all foreign troops from the country. The Lumumba legacy never got abandoned though, as his son, Joseph Kabila succeeded him and governed until January 25, 2019, when Félix Tshisekedi became the new president following his election win the year before. The Kabila team and the team of the new president hammered out a working alliance in early 2019, the result of which is a cabinet-sharing agreement between the Kabila-aligned FCC and Tshisekedi's CACH alliance, which has ensured a continuation in power of the forces that acknowledge Patrice Lumumba's positive role in Congolese history, even if they are failing to live up to the standards he upheld.

The tragic loss of Patrice Lumumba was best expressed by Noam Chomsky during a September 11, 2013, interview with the renowned non-establishment broadcast journalist, syndicated columnist, investigative reporter, and author Amy Goodman whose investigative assignments took her to places like Nigeria and East Timor. He said that:

> *"The murder of Lumumba, in which the U.S. was involved, in the Congo destroyed Africa's major hope for development. Congo is now total horror story, for years,"*

Now, Professor Noam Chomsky who is considered by many as the greatest intellectual alive, is also respected as a great American historian, linguist, philosopher, political activist, cognitive scientist, and social critic whose mastery of analytic philosophy is enviable. So, when he continues going back to Congo to highlight the country's plight as a victim of slavery, colonialism, neocolonialism, the cold war, imperialism, and also of globalism, we get to understand why some pundits view the geopolitical entity as the strangulated heart of Africa whose resources seem to be a curse than a blessing. When he pointed out to his audience that:

> *"The main mineral in your cell phone, coltan [a black metallic ore], comes from the Eastern Congo. Multinational corporations are there exploiting the very rich mineral resources of the region. A lot of them are backing militias which are fighting one other to gain control of the resources or a piece of the resources."*

He underscored the reason why this country that occupies most of the space that is middle or central Africa is the playground of the foreign forces that see in Africa and its rich resources nothing more than booty that can be pillaged at little or no cost by eliminating those determined to defend the interests of the land and the people with impunity, and then replacing them with compradors who would work for foreign interests and their own interests instead, against the interest of their countries and people.

It is hardly three decades ago that Zaire (Congo-Kinshasa) and Cameroon had the reputation for being the only two countries in Africa where those who sacrificed for their liberation or independence had never governed. So the fact that Congolese of the former Belgian Congo managed to overcome their leaders with the evil disposition that were put in place by foreign powers to serve the interests of these alien powers against the welfare of the Congolese people, tells us that the country has come a long way in the difficult journey to reverse the ravages of slavery, colonialism, neocolonialism and imperialism, leaving Cameroon as the only country in Africa with an unfinished liberation that risks tearing the haunted country apart, unless the civic-nationalists of Cameroon act in a timely manner in dismantling the French-imposed system that the regime of Paul Biya manages, in what is generally the degeneration of this geopolitical entity known as the microcosm of Africa.

Democracy Index: Africa and the World

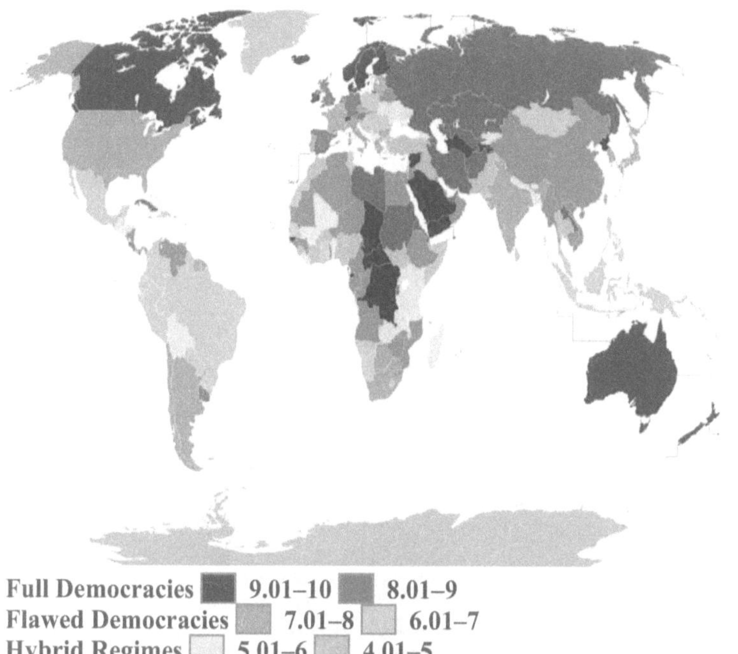

African Countries

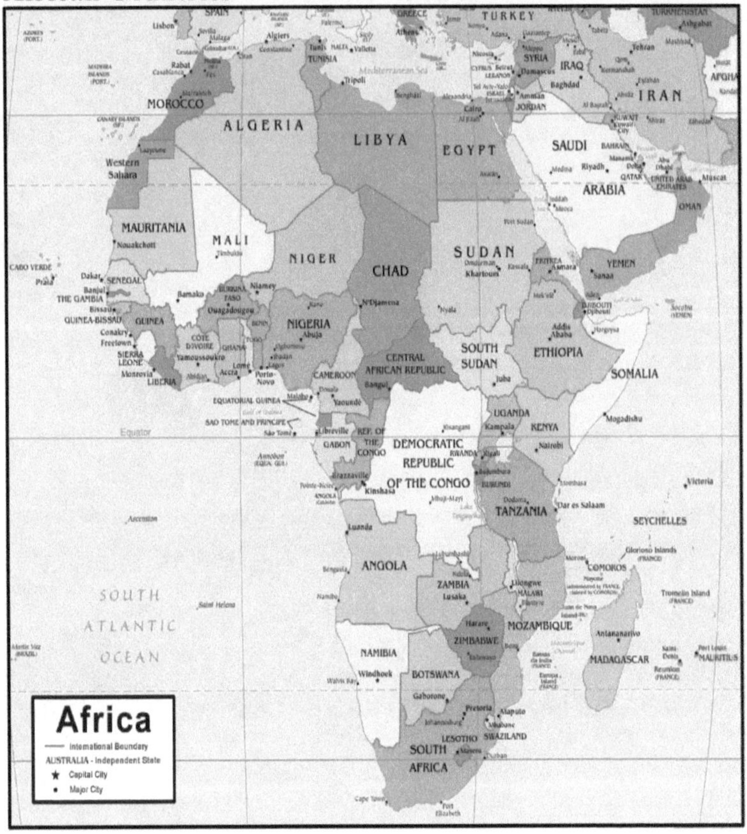

www.ingramcontent.com/pod-product-compliance
Lightning Source LLC
Chambersburg PA
CBHW051424250726
48655CB00003B/1231